ON YOUR MARK

WORKBOOK

2

INTRODUCTORY

Second Edition

Karen Davy

Workbook by Cheryl Pavlik

Longman

On Your Mark 2 Workbook, Second Edition

Pearson Education, 10 Bank Street, White Plains, NY 10606

Vice president, director of publishing: Allen Ascher
Editorial director: Louise Jennewine
Acquisitions editor: Bill Preston
Vice president, director of design and production: Rhea Banker
Development editor: Barbara Barysh
Production manager: Alana Zdinak
Production supervisor: Liza Pleva
Executive managing editor: Linda Moser
Production editor: Lynn Contrucci
Director of manufacturing: Patrice Fraccio
Senior manufacturing buyer: Edith Pullman
Photo research: The Quarasan Group
Cover design: Charles Yuen
Text design and composition: The Quarasan Group
Photo credits: p. 9, PhotoDisc, Inc. (1, 2, 4, 7–12), Comstock, Inc. (3, 5, 6); p. 16,
    Paramount/Picture Quest (1), PhotoDisc, Inc. (3), Corbis (4, 6); p. 25, Image
    provided by MetaTools (1), PhotoDisc, Inc. (2, 7, 9), Corel (3, 6, 8), Comstock,
    Inc. (5); p. 32, Corel (1), PhotoDisc, Inc. (2, 4), Image provided by MetaTools (3);
    p. 37, Emma Lee/Life File/PhotoDisc, Inc. (top), David Turnley/Corbis (center),
    Corbis (bottom); p. 43, Dick Young/Unicorn Stock Photo (top left), Michael
    Newman/PhotoEdit (top right), PhotoDisc, Inc. (bottom); p. 45, Corbis; p. 55,
    Comstock (picture frame); p. 62, PhotoDisc, Inc.; p. 67, Steve Raymer/Corbis (1),
    Color Day Productions/Image Bank (2), Ralph H. Wetmore II/Stone (3),
    Corbis (4); pp. 70, 71, Cartesia (map); p. 93, PhotoDisc, Inc.
Illustrations: Scott Annis p. 11; Chris Celusniak pp. 29, 39, 53, 78; Ruta Daugavietis
    pp. 28, 61, 72, 88; John Faulkner pp. 10, 24, 44, 46; Dennis Franzen pp. 32
    (bottom), 77; Tom Garcia pp. 41, 48; Lane Gregory pp. 34, 90; George Hamblin
    pp. 13, 18, 20, 26, 57, 64, 76 (top), 80; Mitch Heinze pp. 19, 91; Al Hering pp. 21,
    38, 49, 76 (bottom); Jared Lee pp. 42, 55; Tom McKee pp. 50–52, 56, 65, 81, 83,
    89, 94; Philip Scheuer pp. 1, 12, 33; George Ulrich pp. 17, 59, 86; Jim Wisniewski
    pp. 22, 35, 36, 40, 73, 74; John Zielinski pp. 82, 84
Cover photos: Jim Barber/The Stock Rep (keyboard), © 1999 David Lissy, All
    Rights Reserved (runner's foot), © Jim Westphalen (type)

ISBN 0-201-64579-3

1 2 3 4 5 6 7 8 9 10—BAH—06 05 04 03 02 01

PRACTICE 1

Introductions

Work with a partner. Take turns introducing yourselves. Write the conversation.

PRACTICE 2

Things to Say

Ask and answer questions.

    _d_   **1.** What's your name?   **a.** 73 Bank Street

_____ **2.** Where are you from?   **b.** Yes, I do.

_____ **3.** Do you have a phone?   **c.** I'm from Romania.

_____ **4.** What's your address?   **d.** Elena

_____ **5.** How old are you?   **e.** Santa Monica

_____ **6.** What class are you in?   **f.** seventeen

_____ **7.** Where do you live?   **g.** English 101

WHEN IS YOUR BIRTHDAY?

PRACTICE 1

Ordinal Numbers

Complete the chart with the ordinal number or the number word.

Ordinal Number	Number Word	Ordinal Number	Number Word
a. 12th	*twelfth*	**f.**	thirtieth
b. 8th		**g.**	sixth
c.	seventeenth	**h.** 24th	
d. 16th		**i.** 2nd	
e. 21st		**j.**	twenty-seventh

PRACTICE 2

A. Write the names of the months.

1. aym _____May_____
2. tbrooce _____
3. raerufby _____
4. nuej _____
5. yulj _____
6. rjynaua _____

7. uuatsg _____
8. lapri _____
9. eeerdcmb _____
10. cmrah _____
11. vmbeoner _____
12. meespertb _____

B. Complete the sentences with the name of the month or the number word for the ordinal number.

1. June is the _____sixth_____ month of the year.
2. _____ is the twelfth month of the year.
3. August is the _____ month of the year.
4. February is the _____ month of the year.
5. What's the third month of the year? _____
6. What's the tenth month of the year? _____

PRACTICE 3

Look at the month of December. Answer the questions. Use sentences.

DECEMBER						
Sunday	Monday	Tuesday	Wednesday	Thursday	Friday	Saturday
			1	2	3	4
5	6	7	8	9	10 Alma's birthday	11 Alma's party
12	13	14	15	16	17 Tomiko's birthday	18
19	20	21	22	23	24	25
26	27	28	29	30	31	

1. When is Alma's birthday? _____

2. When is Tomiko's birthday? _____

3. When is Alma's party? _____

4. When is your birthday? _____

PRACTICE 4

Ask students in your class, "When is your birthday?" Write the names and the dates on the calendar.

JANUARY	FEBRUARY	MARCH	APRIL
MAY	**JUNE**	**JULY** Paul, 23rd	**AUGUST**
SEPTEMBER	**OCTOBER**	**NOVEMBER**	**DECEMBER**

Example:

KENJI: When is your birthday, Paul?

PAUL: It's on July twenty-third. When is your birthday, Kenji?

PRACTICE 5

Complete the sentences. Use a frequency adverb and the correct form of the verb. (The % tells you the frequency adverb to use.)

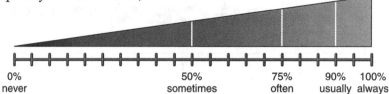

0%	50%	75%	90%	100%
never	sometimes	often	usually	always

1. **100%** I (has/have) _____*always have*_____ cake and ice cream on my birthday.

2. **75%** We (goes/go) _____ to my grandmother's house on Thanksgiving.

3. **50%** Scott (eats/eat) _____ cake and ice cream on the Fourth of July.

4. **90%** Do you (celebrates/celebrate) _____ New Year's Eve with your friends?

5. **0%** My cousins (gives/give) _____ me birthday presents.

PRACTICE 6

Complete the sentences with *There is* or *There are*.

1. _____*There are*_____ thirty-one days in December.

2. _____ a birthday party for Mark on Saturday.

3. _____ a holiday on December 25th.

4. _____ six birthdays in our class in December.

5. _____ seven days in a week.

6. _____ twelve months in a year.

DECEMBER

Sunday	Monday	Tuesday	Wednesday	Thursday	Friday	Saturday
			1	2	3	4
Monica's party 5	6	Ana's birthday 7	8	9	10	Mark's party 11
12	13	14	15	16	17	18
Tina's and Yoko's birthdays 19	20	21	Arturo's birthday 22	23	24	Christmas 25
26	27	28	29	30	31	

PRACTICE 7

Complete the questions with *Is there* or *Are there*. Use the calendar to answer the questions.

Sunday	Monday	Tuesday	Wednesday	Thursday	Friday	Saturday
			1	2	3	4 Inventor Henry Ford's Birthday
5	6 U.S. Labor Day	7 Brazilian Independence Day	8	9	10	11
12	13	14	15 Japanese Respect for the Aged Day	16	17	18
19	20	21	22	23	24	25
26 Poet T. S. Eliot's Birthday	27	28	29	30	31	

SEPTEMBER

1. **A:** _Are there_ thirty-one days in September?

   B: _No, there aren't. There are thirty days in September._

2. **A:** _____ a Japanese holiday in September?

   B: _____

3. **A:** _____ two famous writers' birthdays in September?

   B: _____

4. **A:** _____ a Brazilian holiday on September 30th?

   B: _____

5. **A:** _____ an inventor's birthday in September?

   B: _____

PRACTICE 8

Listen to the conversation. Write the dates of the birthdays.

Name	Birthday
Yuri	
Carol	
Andrew's sister	
Andrew	

Read Peter's letter to Manuel. Then answer the questions. Write complete sentences.

Wednesday, November 24

Dear Manuel,

Hi ! How are you?

Tomorrow is Thanksgiving in the United States. Thanksgiving is always celebrated on the fourth Thursday in November. My family usually goes to my grandmother's house on Thanksgiving. My mother, my sister, and my aunt help my grandmother cook dinner. We always have turkey, stuffing, and sweet potatoes. For dessert we usually have pumpkin pie. We usually eat a lot on Thanksgiving. After dinner, we all play word games and watch football games on TV.

Maybe you can come to the United States to celebrate Thanksgiving with us.

Is there a holiday in your country in November? Please write about it.

Your friend,
Peter

1. When is Thanksgiving?
Thanksgiving is always on the fourth Thursday in November.

2. Where does Peter's family usually go on Thanksgiving?

_____

3. Who usually cooks the Thanksgiving dinner?

_____

4. What does Peter always eat for Thanksgiving dinner?

_____

5. What does Peter's family do after dinner?

_____

PRACTICE 10

Write these sentences correctly. Add capital letters.

1. my name is mike.
My name is Mike.

2. i am seventeen years old.

3. my birthday is on february 14th.

4. this year my birthday is on saturday.

5. it's also valentine's day.

PRACTICE 11

Draw a picture of your favorite holiday and write about it. Tell what you usually do on this holiday. Use the words *always*, *often*, and *sometimes*. Use capital letters correctly.

Check Your Knowledge

Vocabulary Check

Read each sentence. Write the birthday, holiday, or activity on the calendar.

JANUARY

Sunday	Monday	Tuesday	Wednesday	Thursday	Friday	Saturday
	1	2	3	4	5	6
7	8	9	10	11	12	13
14	15	16	17	18	19	20
21	22	23	24	25	26	27
28	29	30	31			

1. Ted's birthday is on the twenty-second.
2. Martin Luther King Day is on the nineteenth.
3. There is a basketball game on the ninth and the sixteenth.
4. New Year's Day is on the first.
5. Susan has band practice on the sixth, the thirteenth, and the twentieth.

Check Your Understanding

A. Complete the sentences. Use a frequency adverb and the correct form of the verb. (The % tells you what frequency adverb to use.)

1. **100%** I (**gives/give**) _____always give_____ my mom a present on Mother's Day.

2. **50%** My friends and I (**wears/wear**) _____ green pins to school on St. Patrick's Day.

3. **0%** We (**goes/go**) _____ to school on Independence Day.

4. **75%** Anita (**visits/visit**) _____ her family on Christmas.

5. **90%** Do you (**gets/get**) _____ candy hearts on Valentine's Day?

B. Complete the conversation with the correct words from the box. Use capital letters correctly.

there's	there is
there are	there isn't
is there	there aren't
are there	

KIM: (1.) _____Is there_____ a holiday on January third?

ELSA: No, (2.) _____. But, (3.) _____ always a holiday on January first.

KIM: Oh. (4.) _____ holidays in the months of May and November?

ELSA: Yes, (5.) _____. But, (6.) _____ any holidays in August.

THE CARROTS LOOK DELICIOUS!

PRACTICE 1

A. Look at the pictures. Write the names of the fruits and vegetables.

1. _____

2. _____

3. _____

4. _____

5. _____

6. _____

7. _____

8. _____

9. _____

10. _____

11. _____

12. _____

B. Write the words from Part A in the correct columns.

Fruits	Vegetables	

A. Do you eat these foods? Write *always, usually, often, sometimes,* or *never.*

	Breakfast	Lunch	Dinner	Snack
eggs				
bread				
fruit				
milk				
potatoes				
fish				
cheese				
meat	*never*	*sometimes*	*usually*	*never*
cereal				
vegetables				

B. Write some sentences about what you eat. Use your answers from Part A.

1. *I usually eat meat for dinner. I never eat it for breakfast.*

2. _____

3. _____

4. _____

5. _____

6. _____

A. Complete the advertisement with the correct amounts. Use words from the box.

Amounts of Food		
loaf	jar	box
carton	bag	can(s)
package	pound(s)	bottle

SUPERFOOD SUPERMARKET

Farmgood Milk

1. a _____ for $.79

Aunt Mary's Soups

2. three _____ for $1.50

Apples

3. a _____ for $.69

Idaho Potatoes

4. a _____ for $.89

Yummy Potato Chips

5. a _____ for $1.59

Low-Fat Sugar Cookies

6. a _____ for $1.69

Homestead Bread

7. a _____ for $1.19

Sunnydew Orange Juice

8. a _____ for $2.45

Dairy Fresh Eggs

9. a _____ for $1.49

Chococrunch Cereal

10. a _____ for $2.29

Nutty Time Peanut Butter

11. a _____ for $1.99

Sweet 'n' Spicy Beans

12. a _____ for $.79

B. What are you buying today? Write each food. How much does it cost?

Item	Cost
bottle of juice	$2.45
_____	_____
_____	_____
_____	_____

C. You have $5. How much are all the items in Part B? Do you get change? How much?

Total: $_____   Change: $_____

Look at the picture. Write questions and answers with *some* and *any*.

Examples:

A: Do they have any **eggs**?

A: Yes, they have some **eggs**.

B: Do they have any **meat**?

B: No, they don't have any **meat**.

1. soup   A: _____ ?

             B: _____ .

2. fruit   A: _____ ?

             B: _____ .

3. chicken   A: _____ ?

             B: _____ .

4. potatoes A: _____ ?

             B: _____ .

5. cereal   A: _____ ?

             B: _____ .

Listen to the names of the foods. Write them in the correct list.

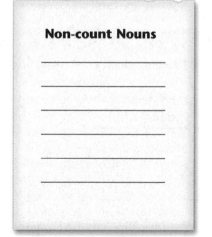

Count Nouns	Non-count Nouns
_____	_____
_____	_____
_____	_____
_____	_____
_____	_____
_____	_____

Complete the conversation. Write *How much* or *How many*.

MARTIN: Help me make a shopping list, Lee.

(1.) _____ milk do we need?

LEE: We have about a cup. We need another carton.

MARTIN: (2.) _____ oranges do we have?

LEE: We have two oranges. Let's buy more.

MARTIN: (3.) _____ chicken do you need

for lunch this week?

LEE: Oh, about three or four pieces for sandwiches.

MARTIN: (4.) _____ tomatoes do we have?

LEE: We have one tomato. Let's get some more.

I'd like some corn and carrots, too.

MARTIN: OK. (5.) _____ juice is there?

LEE: There's a carton of orange juice. I think

we're OK, Dad.

MARTIN: Thanks, Lee. Let's go to the store now.

Read the menu and the Food Guide Pyramid. Answer the questions.

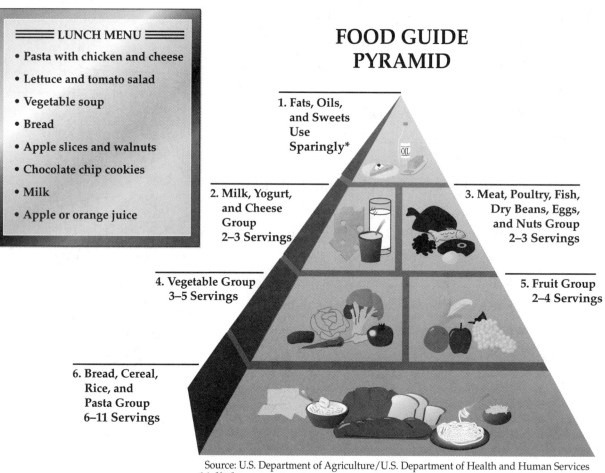

LUNCH MENU
- Pasta with chicken and cheese
- Lettuce and tomato salad
- Vegetable soup
- Bread
- Apple slices and walnuts
- Chocolate chip cookies
- Milk
- Apple or orange juice

FOOD GUIDE PYRAMID

1. Fats, Oils, and Sweets Use Sparingly*

2. Milk, Yogurt, and Cheese Group 2–3 Servings

3. Meat, Poultry, Fish, Dry Beans, Eggs, and Nuts Group 2–3 Servings

4. Vegetable Group 3–5 Servings

5. Fruit Group 2–4 Servings

6. Bread, Cereal, Rice, and Pasta Group 6–11 Servings

Source: U.S. Department of Agriculture/U.S. Department of Health and Human Services
*A little amount

1. Which menu items are in food group 1?

   _____

2. Which menu items are in food group 2?

   _____

3. Which menu items are in food group 3?

   _____

4. Which menu items are in food group 4?

   _____

5. Which menu items are in food group 5?

   _____

6. Which menu items are in food group 6?

   _____

PRACTICE 8

Add punctuation marks to these sentences.

1. What do we need from the supermarket
2. We need milk cheese and bread
3. Ralph likes cereal with banana for breakfast but he doesn't like orange juice
4. Suki didn't have any food in her refrigerator so she went to her friend's house for dinner
5. Paul's doctor says to eat a healthy snack and drink a lot of milk every day
6. Leo eats four pieces of bread for breakfast every morning

PRACTICE 9

Look at the food pyramid on page 14. What is your favorite food group? Write about your favorite foods and your favorite meal.

 **Check Your Knowledge**

Vocabulary Check

Look at the pictures. Write the names and the amounts of food.

1. _____   2. _____   3. _____

4. _____   5. _____   6. _____

Check Your Understanding

A. Tom and Alicia are at the supermarket. Complete their conversation with *how much*, *how many*, *some*, or *any*. Use capital letters correctly.

Tom:	(1.) _____ soup do we need?
Alicia:	Three cans.
Tom:	Do we have (2.) _____ fruit?
Alicia:	Yes. We have (3.) _____ apples.
Tom:	Oh, I want (4.) _____ cookies, too.
Alicia:	But, we don't need (5.) _____ cookies. We have five boxes at home. Do you want (6.) _____ vegetables?
Tom:	Yes. I'd like (7.) _____ peppers for a salad.
Alicia:	(8.) _____ do you want?
Tom:	Let's buy three.
Alicia:	OK. That's it! (9.) _____ money do you have?
Tom:	Oh, I thought *you* had (10.) _____ money!

B. Add punctuation to these sentences.

1. How many potatoes do you want

2. My sister always eats cereal fruit and bread for breakfast

3. Do you like pizza with cheese or do you like pizza without cheese

4. I'm really hungry so let's make a lot of sandwiches for lunch

WHAT DO YOU HAVE TO DO TODAY?

PRACTICE 1

Look at the pictures. Complete the sentences with the correct words from the box.

breakfast	morning
lunch	afternoon
dinner	evening
snack	

1. Dan eats _____ at 7:00 in the _____.

2. Barbara is always hungry after school. She has a _____ at four o'clock in the _____.

3. At noon, Tara eats _____ in the cafeteria.

4. Sam and Yoko have _____ at 6:30 in the _____.

PRACTICE 2

Work with a partner. Ask these questions. Write your partner's answers. Use complete sentences.

1. When do you have breakfast?
   Kate always has breakfast at 7:00 in the morning.

2. When do you have lunch?
   _____

3. What time do you usually have a snack?
   _____

4. When do you have dinner?
   _____

Look at these pictures of Kate. Match the sentences with the pictures.

_____e____ **1.** She leaves for school.   _____ **5.** She gets dressed.

_____ **2.** She has breakfast.   _____ **6.** She takes a shower.

_____ **3.** She eats dinner.   _____ **7.** She brushes her hair.

_____ **4.** She gets up.   _____ **8.** She brushes her teeth.

a.

b.

c.

d.

e.

f.

g.

h.

Complete the sentences about Vicki's morning routine. Write *before* or *after*. Use capital letters, if needed.

Vicki's Daily Routine

1. _____ I get dressed, I take a shower.

2. _____ I get dressed, I eat breakfast.

3. _____ I go to school, I comb my hair.

4. I always brush my teeth _____ I leave for school.

5. I go home _____ my science class.

6. I watch television _____ I do my homework.

Read the sentences. Write one sentence using *before* or *after*.

1. Sam gets up. Then he gets dressed.
   After Sam gets up, he gets dressed. _____

2. Sam eats breakfast. Then he leaves for school.
   _____

3. Sam has English class in the morning. He has lunch at noon.
   _____

4. Sam has band practice. Then he goes home.
   _____

5. Sam eats dinner with his family. Then he watches TV.
   _____

PRACTICE 6

Complete the sentences with the correct forms
of *go, go to,* or *go to the.*

My name is Susana Hernandez. I **(1.)** _____
Westgate School. I am very busy. In the morning, I
(2.) _____ science class. At 11:00, I
(3.) _____ Student Center and have a snack
with my friends. Then I **(4.)** _____ my art
classes in the afternoon.

After classes, I **(5.)** _____
downtown with my friend, Alex. We usually
(6.) _____ coffee shop to eat
dinner, but sometimes I **(7.)** _____
my grandmother's house. In the evening, I **(8.)** _____ library. Then I
(9.) _____ home and **(10.)** _____ bed.

PRACTICE 7

Complete the following sentences with the correct forms of *have to.*

1. _____*Does*_____ Susumu _____*have to*_____ go to class at 8:00? Yes, he
   does. He _____*has to*_____ get up now.

2. _____ Alma and Mike _____ go to swim practice
   this morning? Yes, they do, and they _____ eat breakfast first.

3. Don _____ go to school five days a week. He doesn't
   _____ go to class on Saturday.

4. Gloria and Ann _____ do a lot of homework tonight. They
   _____ do it before they watch television.

5. Allen _____ leave at 6:45 every morning. He _____
   get to work early.

6. It's late. I _____ leave now. I _____ be home by 9:00.

PRACTICE 8

What do students in your school have to do? Check (✓) the correct box.
Then write sentences.

Students in my school...	have to	don't have to
1. eat lunch in the cafeteria	✓	
2. go to school on Saturday		
3. study a language		
4. play sports		
5. do a lot of homework		
6. go to school in July		

1. _Students in my school have to eat lunch in the cafeteria._

2. _____

3. _____

4. _____

5. _____

6. _____

PRACTICE 9

Listen to Edna's daily routine. Write what she does.

In the morning	In the afternoon	In the evening
gets up		

Read about Kenji's busy schedule. Answer the questions. Use complete sentences.

Dear Ali,

Thanks for inviting me to your house for the weekend. I'm sorry, but I can't go because I'm very busy this weekend. On Saturday morning, I have to go to soccer practice. Our team is really good this year and I'm the captain! I'm sending you a picture of my team.

In the afternoon, I have to eat lunch with my grandmother. Then I have to wash my father's car. After that, I have to go to the library and study for my history test.

I have to stay home with my little brother and sister on Saturday night, too. On Sunday, I have to go to a baseball game with my cousin, Yoshio.

Please write next week. I miss you very much.

Kenji

1. What does Kenji have to do on Saturday morning?

   _____

2. What does he have to do after lunch?

   _____

3. When will Kenji study for his history test?

   _____

4. What does he have to do on Saturday night?

   _____

5. When will Kenji go to the baseball game?

   _____

PRACTICE 11

Complete the sentences with *and, but, so,* or *because*. Write a comma, if needed.

1. In the morning I have a shower _____ I get dressed before I eat breakfast.

2. I can't go to the movies _____ I have to study.

3. My parents aren't at home _____ I have to stay home with my little sister.

4. At my school, we don't have uniforms _____ we have to wear black pants and a white shirt.

5. Paula gets bad grades _____ she never studies.

6. Kim has to go to school _____ I don't.

PRACTICE 12

Your friend asked you to go to a party, but you can't go. What do you have to do? Write a letter to your friend.

_____

_____

_____

_____

_____

_____

_____

_____

_____

_____

_____

Check Your Knowledge

Vocabulary Check

Complete the sentences with the correct words from the box. Use the correct verb form.

brush his teeth	read the newspaper	get up
get dressed	have dinner	have breakfast
go to bed	comb his hair	take a shower

1. Every morning, Tony _____ at 7:00.

2. Then he _____.

3. Then he _____.

4. Then he _____.

5. Then he _____ and _____.

Check Your Understanding

A. Look at the pictures in **Vocabulary Check**. Use the words to complete the sentences about Tony.

    1. (get up) After _____.

    2. (have breakfast) Before _____.

B. What do you have to do each day? Write sentences with *have to* for each time of day.

    1. 7:00 a.m. _____.

    2. 10:00 a.m. _____.

    3. after school _____.

PRACTICE 1

brush	magazine
compact disc (CD)	cassette
newspaper	toothpaste
toothbrush	video
comb	

A. Look at the pictures. Write the correct word(s) from the box.

1. _____ 2. _____ 3. _____

4. _____ 5. _____ 6. _____

7. _____ 8. _____ 9. _____

B. Complete the sentences. Use words from Part A.

1. Sometimes you can buy a _____*newspaper*_____ at a bookstore.
2. At the drugstore you can always buy some toothpaste and a _____, a _____ and a _____.
3. I saw a great _____ about new cars at the bookstore.
4. The music store sells a lot of good _____ and _____, but it doesn't have any _____ to rent.

Look at the picture. Complete the sentences with *one* or *some* and the name of the store.

1. **A:** Where can I buy milk?

   B: You can buy _____*some*_____ at ___*Tom's Grocery*___.

2. **A:** I need a comb.

   B: You can get _____ at _____.

3. **A:** I need six eggs for Mandy's cake.

   B: You can buy _____ at _____.

4. **A:** I don't have any money.

   B: You can get _____ at _____.

5. **A:** Frank wants a new CD.

   B: He can get _____ at _____.

6. **A:** The car needs gas. Where can I get _____?

   B: At the _____.

7. **A:** Do you have today's newspaper?

   B: Sorry, I don't. But you can buy _____
   at _____.

8. **A:** Where can I buy a new brush?

   B: You can get _____ at _____.

PRACTICE 3

Complete the sentences with the verb and infinitive. Use *don't* or *doesn't*, if needed.

1. She **(want/go)** _____wants to go_____ to the party, but she
   (want/dance) _doesn't want to dance_ .

2. We don't like Italian food, so we **(want/eat)** _____ at Pasta Heaven.

3. Do you **(want/go)** _____ to dinner tonight?

4. They **(want/have)** _____ lunch because they're not hungry.

5. He's sick, so he **(want/go)** _____ to school.

6. I **(want/go)** _____ to the music store because I
   (want/buy) _____ a CD for my sister.

PRACTICE 4

Use the words and *do* or *does* to make questions. Then answer the questions.

1. do/you/want/study/tonight
   Do you want to study tonight?
   Yes, I do **OR** _No I don't._

2. does/your best friend/want/study/with you
   _____
   _____

3. what/your teacher/want/do/after school
   _____
   _____

4. when/they/need/leave
   _____
   _____

5. where/you/want/go/tomorrow
   _____
   _____

6. why/your sister/need/go/to the library
   _____
   _____

Look at the pictures. Complete the sentences with *this*, *these*, *that*, or *those*.

1. I'd like to buy _____ magazine.

2. How much are _____ shoes?

3. I want to buy _____ CDs.

4. I'd like to rent _____ video, please.

5. _____ combs are mine, too.

6. Can I rent _____ video for two days?

7. Michael's photograph is in

_____ newspaper.

8. Are _____ books yours?

PRACTICE 6

Listen to the conversations. Circle the correct answers.

Conversation 1

1. What does Lucy want to buy?
   a. a present for her mother
   b. a card for her mother

2. How much money does Lucy have?
   a. a lot
   b. a little

3. What is the name of the store Maria likes?
   a. The Fashion Place
   b. Women's Clothing Store

4. Where is it?
   a. on Post Street
   b. near the post office

Conversation 2

1. Where is Dan going?
   a. to Mexico
   b. to the mall

2. What does he want to buy?
   a. a book about Mexico
   b. a book in Spanish

3. Where does Sue tell Dan to go?
   a. to Baker's Bookstore
   b. to Worldwide Books

4. Where is the store?
   a. on Front Street
   b. in the mall

PRACTICE 7

Look at the map. Answer the questions.

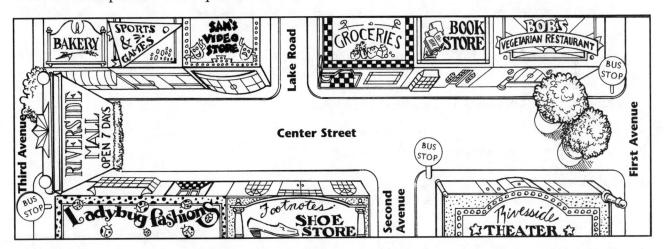

1. What's the name of the shopping mall? _____

2. Where can you go to eat fruits and vegetables? _____

3. Where does the bus stop? _____

4. What's the name of the video store? _____

5. Where is the shoe store? _____

6. What's next to the bakery? _____

Look at the advertisements. Read about the stores. Answer the questions.

1. How many U-Rent-It Video stores are there in Oakville?

   _____

2. What kinds of books are on sale at the bookstore?

   _____

3. What items are on sale at the drugstore?

   _____

4. Is there a sale at Mega Music this Wednesday?

   _____

5. Which stores are in the Oaks Mall?

   _____

6. Where is Bicycle Adventure?

   _____

PRACTICE 9

Rewrite these sentences. Use capitalization correctly.

1. history class begins at Eight. _____

2. i don't go to School on saturday. _____

3. please give marta this Book. _____

4. My birthday is in march. _____

5. Did You tell the Teacher? _____

6. she lives in new york city. _____

PRACTICE 10

A.   Draw a map of your favorite mall. Write the name of the mall and the names of the stores, streets, and avenues.

B.   Write about your mall. What's the name of your mall? Where are the stores? What do the stores sell, and what's on sale?

My favorite mall is _____ . _____ _has a lot of children's books._

This week the picture books are on sale. _____

_____

_____

_____

_____

Check Your Knowledge

Vocabulary Check

Complete the sentences. Use the pictures and some words from the box.

Things to Buy	Places
apples	music store
cassette	bookstore
comb	drugstore
gas	video store
video	gas station
magazine	grocery store

1. Teresa wants to buy a _____.
   She needs to go to the _____.

2. Pablo wants to buy a _____.
   He needs to go to the _____.

3. Teng needs some _____ for his car. He needs
   to go to the _____.

4. I want to buy some _____. I need to go
   to the _____.

5. Sandra wants a _____. She needs to go to
   the _____.

Check Your Understanding

Look at the map. Choose two places to go to. Why do you need to go to those places? Where are they on the map? Write a paragraph.

Music Store   Video Store   Gas Station   Grocery Store   Drugstore   PARK AVENUE   4TH STREET

_____

_____

_____

_____

PRACTICE 1

Look at the pictures. Complete the sentences with the correct words from the box.

car	garage
house	wallet
apartment	on fire
bike	truck
ambulance	accident

1. Did you see someone next to my _____ today? A burglar broke into it.

2. Oh, no! Someone stole my car. It was in my _____ last night.

3. Please hurry! Our _____ is on fire. It's at 411 Elm Street.

4. That man stole my _____!

5. A little girl fell off her _____. She was really hurt. The _____ came a few minutes after a neighbor called the emergency operator.

6. Look! That's a terrible _____! Is anyone hurt?

7. Can't you find your _____?

8. My neighbor's _____ is _____!

Look at the pictures. Complete the conversations with the correct words from the box.

accident	ambulance
bleeding	breathe
broke	choking
emergency	fell

MRS. RUIZ: My daughter just had an

(1.) _____. She

(2.) _____ out of a tree.

She's (3.) _____, and

I think she (4.) _____

her leg.

OPERATOR: Where are you?

MRS. RUIZ: At 497 Oakcrest Road.

OPERATOR: Stay calm! An (5.) _____

will be there in five minutes.

MRS. RUIZ: OK. Thank you!

OPERATOR: This is the 911 operator. Can I help

you?

MRS. SANTO: Yes, it's an (6.) _____.

My husband is (7.) _____.

He can't (8.) _____.

OPERATOR: Where are you now?

MRS. SANTO: De Palma's Restaurant, on Center

Street.

OPERATOR: Someone will be there soon!

MRS. SANTO: Thanks!

broke into	fell down
get up	picked up
ran into	took out

Complete the sentences with the correct two-word verbs from the box.

1. I _____ the tree.

2. I can't _____!

3. I _____ again!

4. I _____ your pencil. It was on the floor.

5. I _____ a dollar from my wallet to pay the bus fare.

6. A burglar _____ my apartment!

PRACTICE 4

Complete the chart with the past tense form of the verb.

Simple Present Tense	Simple Past Tense	Simple Present Tense	Simple Past Tense
1. call		**6.** see	
2. happen		**7.** go	
3. break		**8.** fall	
4. run		**9.** take	
5. get		**10.** hit	

PRACTICE 5

Complete the sentences with the simple present or past tense form of the verbs.

1. We (see) _____ a good movie last night.

2. Yesterday I (go) _____ home after school.

3. My friends (come) _____ for lunch every Saturday.

4. She (fall) _____ down and hurt her head last Saturday.

5. Frank's teacher is angry because he never (get) _____ to class on time.

6. We (take) _____ the train to New York last year.

7. Oh, no! I don't have any money. Someone (steal) _____ my wallet!

8. Please be careful. Don't (break) _____ the glass.

PRACTICE 6

Write the simple present or past tense form of the verbs. Remember to use *did* in past tense questions.

PILAR:	When (1. break) _____ Phal _____ his arm?
DAUDI:	He (2. break) _____ it last Saturday. I was with him.
PILAR:	What (3. happen) _____?
DAUDI:	He (4. fall) _____ off his bike.
PILAR:	How (5. happen) _____ that _____?

DAUDI: We (6. ride) _____ our bikes to the park. We didn't see the cat run next to him. He almost hit it. I (7. see) _____ him fall.

PILAR: What (8. do) _____ you _____?

DAUDI: I (9. call) _____ my neighbor. She came in her car and (10. take) _____ us to the emergency room at Jefferson Hospital. He feels better now.

Listen. Answer the questions about the emergency telephone calls.

Caller 1

1. Who did Fran call?

   _____

2. Why did Fran make the call?

   _____

3. Who is coming to help Fran?

   _____

Caller 2

1. Why did Michael call 911?

   _____

2. What happened to Juan?

   _____

3. Where did the accident happen?

   _____

4. When is the ambulance coming?

   _____

Caller 3

1. Why did Angelina call 911?

   _____

2. Where is she calling from?

   _____

3. What's the name of the restaurant?

   _____

Read the accident report. Write the answers to the questions.

Westlake School
Accident Report

Person reporting :
Celia Benner, School Nurse

Date:
September 14

Time:
10:30 a.m.

Location:
Westlake School, library

Patient's name:
Ann Tomasic

Teacher's name:
Maya Chang, librarian

What happened?   Ann wanted to get a book from the top shelf. She fell off the ladder. She hit her head and hurt her arm. The librarian, Ms. Chang, called me immediately. When I got to the library, Ann was on the floor. She wasn't bleeding, but she said that her arm hurt a lot. I called her mother. Mrs. Tomasic picked her up at 11 and took her to County General Hospital.

Injuries: Dr. Fields reported that Ann broke her arm.

1. Who was hurt? _____
2. Where was the accident? _____
3. When did the accident happen? _____
4. How did the accident happen? _____
5. What was Ann's injury? _____
6. Who filled out the accident report? _____

PRACTICE 9

Look at the pictures. Write one sentence for each picture.

1. _____

_____

2. _____

_____

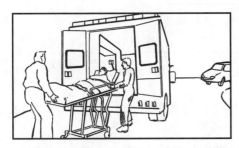

3. _____

_____

4. _____

_____

PRACTICE 10

What happened to the boy in Practice 9? Write a paragraph. Use the pictures and sentences from Practice 9. Add more sentences to tell *what* happened, *where* it happened, *when* it happened, and *why* it happened.

_____

_____

_____

_____

_____

_____

_____

_____

_____

Check Your Knowledge

Vocabulary Check

Complete the sentences with the correct words from the box.

accident	apartment	breathe	broke
burglar	car	choking	fell off
garage	on fire	purse	truck

1.   2.   3.   4.

1. A _____ stole my sister's _____.

2. Our _____ is _____!

3. Help! Judy is _____. She can't _____!

4. Tim _____ his bike. He _____ his arm.

Check Your Understanding

A. Complete the paragraph with the simple past tense form of each verb.

Mario **(1. see)** _____ a car accident yesterday. A small car

(2. hit) _____ a big car. He **(3. run)** _____ to

a phone and **(4. call)** _____ 911. Then an ambulance

(5. take) _____ the people in the accident to the hospital.

B. These sentences are about Daniel's bike accident, but they are not in the correct order. Number the sentences from 1 to 5. Then use the information to complete the accident report.

_____ The car hit Daniel Palmer's bike.

_____ An ambulance took him to Franklin Hospital.

_____ Daniel fell off the bike.

_____ Daniel's hands and arms were bleeding and his right leg hurt.

_____ On March 15 at 2:00 p.m., a car turned from Wilson Street onto Glen Avenue.

Franklin Hospital	**EMERGENCY ROOM REPORT**
Patient's name:	What happened? _____
Date:	_____
Time:	
Location:	Injuries _____

PRACTICE 1

Look at the pictures. Complete the sentences with the correct words from the box.

assembly	auditorium
band	dance
election	science fair
student council	volleyball game

1. What did Janet do for the _____?

2. No one is in the _____ now.

3. The students are at an _____.

4. The _____ meets every Wednesday at 2:30.

5. Kong won the class _____.

6. Emilio plays in a _____.

7. Mark is at a _____.

8. María and David are at a _____.

Make sentences. Match the sentences with the pictures. Then write the sentences under the pictures.

The band	marched	for treasurer.
My sister	danced	the art fair.
We	entered	in the election.
Victor	ran	the gym.
The student council	voted	for the team.
Alexa	decorated	to the music.
All the students	cheered	the assembly.
Laura	attended	at the game.

1. _Victor danced to the music._

2. _____

3. _____

4. _____

5. _____

6. _____

7. _____

8. _____

PRACTICE 3

I	you	he	she
it	we	they	me
him	her	us	them

Complete the conversation with the correct pronouns from the box.

MARCOS: Hey, Win! Where's Yuri?

WIN: **(1.)** _____ is in the first row with Tom and

(2.) _____. Do you want to come and sit with

(3.) _____?

MARCOS: Sure. Hey, I didn't see the first race. Who won **(4.)** _____?

WIN: Tony did. They gave **(5.)** _____ a blue ribbon.

MARCOS: Look! There's my sister Mercedes. **(6.)** _____ is on the

track team this year.

WIN: She's fast, too. I saw

(7.) _____ win at

last week's meet. Marcos, did

(8.) _____ see Paul

and Kenny?

MARCOS: No, **(9.)** _____.

didn't see **(10.)** _____.

Why?

WIN: Do you think **(11.)** _____

want to sit with us, too?

MARCOS: Oh! Let's go find **(12.)** _____.

PRACTICE 4

Complete the chart with simple present or simple past tense verbs.

Simple Present Tense	Simple Past Tense
1. cook	
2.	voted
3. go	
4. study	
5.	marched
6. dance	
7. run	
8. watch	
9.	attended
10. decorate	

PRACTICE 5

Look at the pictures. What did Adam do yesterday? Complete the sentences with
the simple past tense of the verbs. Use *didn't* if the sentence doesn't have a picture.

1. Adam _____ran_____ a race.

2. Adam ___didn't play___ soccer.

3. He _____ in the band.

4. He _____ in the election.

5. He _____ an assembly.

6. He _____ volleyball.

7. He _____ for his math test.

8. He _____ at the basketball
game.

Complete the conversations. Write yes/no questions using the simple past tense.

1. **A:** <u>*Did Paul attend the assembly?*</u>

   B: No, he didn't attend the assembly. He went to science class.

2. **A:** _____?

   B: Yes, I did. It was a great game.

3. **A:** _____?

   B: No, the band didn't play at the game. They played at the assembly.

4. **A:** _____?

   B: No, we didn't cook. We ate dinner at a restaurant.

5. **A:** _____?

   B: Yes, she did. She studied for two hours.

PRACTICE 7

Listen to the conversation. What did Nick, Vanessa, Victor, and Marta do on the weekend? Check (✓) their activities.

	Nick	**Vanessa**	**Victor**	**Marta**
Played in a soccer game				
Decorated for a party				
Cooked for a party				
Went to a party				
Worked in a restaurant				
Did homework				
Cleaned the house				

Read the article. Answer the questions.

Three Cheers for the School Show!

Jenner High School had a special show in the auditorium last Friday night. The students decorated the stage with colored ribbons and balloons.

The Jenner High School band started off the show with an American folk song. Then they played three more folk songs. One song was from Germany, one was from Chile, and the last was from South Africa. The students in the band were dressed in new uniforms. They looked great! After that, the Folk Dance Club danced to the band music. Finally, students from the Music Club came on stage. They played the piano, flute, and violin. At the end of the show, María Azueta and Jason Lee sang a song called "The Band Plays On." Quang Nguyen played the piano for them.

"This show was the best ever," said Principal Muñoz. "The students did a great job!" Congratulations to all the students!

uniform

1. Who started off the school show?

_____

2. What did they do?

_____

3. Where was the show?

_____

4. When was the show?

_____

5. How were the students in the band dressed?

_____

6. What other groups were in the show?

_____

PRACTICE 9

Correct these sentences. Add subjects, capital letters, and pronouns.

1. ben works all day and goes to school at night.

_____

2. norma lives in colombia. is fifteen years old.

_____

3. brought me the book on Tuesday. was interesting.

_____

4. my family went to Mexico in july. had a good time.

_____

PRACTICE 10

Use these notes to write a newspaper article for the Bennett High School newspaper. Use the simple past tense and make sure each sentence has a subject.

When:	*Friday night*
What:	*basketball game*
Where:	*gym*
Who:	*students*
What happened:	*Bennett High School—67/Hillside High School—66 (great game)*

_____

_____

_____

_____

_____

_____

_____

_____

_____

_____

☑ Check Your Knowledge

attended	band
decorated	election
marched	ran
science fair	student council
volleyball	voted

Vocabulary Check

Look at the pictures. Complete the story about Marta's day. Use words from the box.

Yesterday Marta **(1.)** _____ a **(2.)** _____ meeting.

Then she **(3.)** _____ in an **(4.)** _____. After that, she

went to PE class. In PE class she played **(5.)** _____. After school,

Marta **(6.)** _____ in the **(7.)** _____. In the evening, she

(8.) _____ the gym with her friends.

Check Your Understanding

A. Complete the conversation. Write the simple past tense. Use *did* or *didn't* if needed.

A: What **(1. do)** _____ you _____ after school yesterday?

B: I **(2. go)** _____ to band practice. We **(3. march)** _____ twelve blocks up the street.
I was so tired, but in the evening, I **(4. attend)** _____ a school meeting and then
I **(5. go)** _____ to the school dance. **(6. go)** _____ you _____ to the dance?

A: No, I **(7. go)** _____ to the dance. I **(8. study)** _____ for the big English test.

B. Use these notes. Write an article in your notebook about the school dance..

What happened?	*a school dance*
When and where did it happen?	*Friday 7:00 p.m., Lincoln High School gym*
Who was there?	*Lincoln High students, their teachers, and their parents*

Look at the picture. Read the descriptions. Write the person's name.

a. _____ **b.** _____ **c.** _____ **d.** _____ **e.** _____ **f.** _____

1. Paul is tall and thin. He has straight black hair. He's wearing shorts and a sweater.

2. Debbie is short and thin. She has long black hair. She's wearing a long white skirt, a white hat, and sunglasses.

3. Phil is tall and heavy. He has wavy hair. He's wearing black pants and a white sweater.

4. Carl is tall and thin. He has curly hair. He's wearing jeans and a T-shirt.

5. Maggie is short and thin. She has short, straight black hair. She's wearing white pants and a white T-shirt.

6. Sarah is short and heavy. Her hair is short and straight. She is wearing glasses.

Look at the pictures. Complete the stories with the correct forms of *be, have,* and *wear.*

A. My name is Carl. I **(1.)** _____
short for my age and of average weight.
Right now I **(2.)** _____ really short hair.

B. Molly, Emily, and Cass are sisters. Cass
(3.) _____ tall, and she
(4.) _____ long wavy hair.
Molly **(5.)** _____ short, and Emily
(6.) _____ of average height.
Molly and Emily **(7.)** _____ short,
straight hair. All three girls **(8.)** _____ thin.

C. The Sánchez family is from Mexico. Mr. and
Mrs. Sánchez **(9.)** _____ of average
height and weight. Mrs. Sánchez's daughter
(10.) _____ wavy hair.
She **(11.)** _____ tall for her age.
Her brother **(12.)** _____ tall, too.
He **(13.)** _____ short, straight black hair,
and he **(14.)** _____ glasses.

D. Carlos and I are best friends, but we
(15.) _____ very different.
I **(16.)** _____ short and thin, and
he **(17.)** _____ tall and heavy.
I **(18.)** _____ curly hair and Carlos
(19.) _____ short hair.
We **(20.)** _____ the same glasses, but
I wear them to read and Carlos wears his glasses
to play basketball.

Look at the pictures. Write descriptions of the people. Use adjectives in the
correct order. Use the present tense and the present progressive tense.

Cindy   Millie   Gregory   Henry

1. Cindy *has long, wavy hair. She is wearing a short black skirt and a*
   white sweater.

2. Millie _____

   _____

3. Gregory _____

   _____

4. Henry _____

   _____

Look at the pictures. Write sentences. Use the adjectives in the correct order. Use commas if needed.

1. Michelle/short/heavy/girl

   Michelle is a short, heavy girl.

2. Mr. Fernández/black/curly/hair

3. That/white/nice/jacket

4. Aida/thin/pretty/girl

5. Kay/wavy/long/hair

6. Frank/dark/big/eyes

7. Those/pretty/white/socks

Peter	Sam
Jane	Ann

Listen to the conversations. Write the name under the person described.

a. _____ b. _____ c. _____ d. _____ e. _____ f. _____

PRACTICE 6

Look at the picture in Practice 5. Two people don't have names. Describe the people and give them names. Use complete sentences and adjectives in the correct order.

Girl

_____

_____

_____

Boy

_____

_____

_____

Katrina is coming to the United States to visit Angela Johnson and her family.
Read the letter she wrote about herself. Then answer the questions.

August 12, _____

Dear Angela,

How are you? I'm getting ready to come to your house next month.
In your last letter, you asked me to describe myself so you can find me at
the airport. Here's what I look like.

I am tall for my age. My mom says I'm thin, too. I have brown hair and
brown eyes. Right now, my hair is very long. It's also curly. I wear glasses,
but I don't like them.

I like to listen to music. I usually have my CD player with me when I
travel. I also like to dance. Do you have any school dances in the United
States? I hope so!

I'm excited to meet you. I have told my friends that we are pen pals.
Please write to me and tell me more about your family. Then I can look
for you at the airport, too!

Your pen pal,

Katrina Agon

1. Is Katrina tall or short? _____

2. Is she thin or heavy? _____

3. What does her hair look like? _____

4. What does Katrina like to do? _____

5. What does Katrina ask Angela to do? _____

Look at the picture of the Johnson family. Write descriptions of each person.

Mr. Johnson: _short, curly black hair; wears glasses; of average height and weight_

Mrs. Johnson: _____

Angela Johnson: _____

Neal Johnson: _____

PRACTICE 9

Pretend that you are Angela or Neal Johnson. Write a letter to Katrina Agon.
Describe yourself and the people in your family. Write today's date.

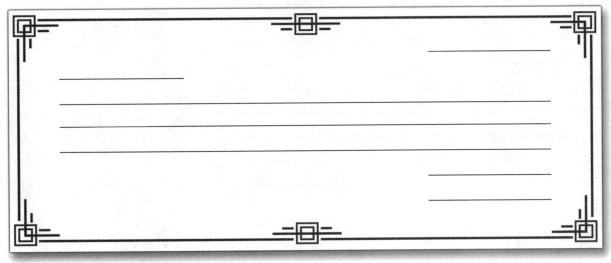

Check Your Knowledge

Vocabulary Check

Look at the people. Describe them. Use words from the box.

average	short	curly
straight	glasses	tall
heavy	thin	long
wavy		

1. Pierre is _____ and

_____.

2. Alma is _____ and

_____.

She has _____,

_____ hair.

3. Tom is of _____ height.

He is a little _____.

4. Dalia has _____ hair.

She wears _____.

Check Your Understanding

A. Complete the sentences about Anita with two adjectives from the box. Write the adjectives in the correct order. Use each word only one time.

blue	curly
long	pretty
tall	thin

1. Anita is a _____ _____ woman.

2. She has _____ _____ hair.

3. She is wearing a _____ _____ sweater.

B. Write a description of Paul or Tina. Describe the person's personal appearance and clothing. Use colors to describe the clothing.

_____

_____

_____

_____

_____

_____

_____

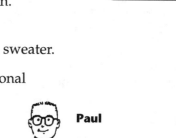

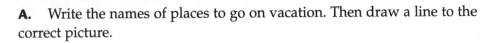

HOW WAS YOUR VACATION?

PRACTICE 1

A. Write the names of places to go on vacation. Then draw a line to the correct picture.

1. l e l a t b

<u>b</u> <u>a</u> <u>l</u> <u>l</u> <u>e</u> (t)

2. m m s u u e

○ — ○ — ○ —

3. t h o e l

— ○ — — —

4. c n o e a

— — — — ○

5. c e b a h

— — ○ — —

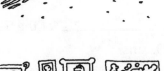

B. Write the letters with circles.

— — — — — — —

C. Read the question. Use the letters in Part B to complete the answer. Write the name of a vacation activity.

Where did the Vegas family go on vacation?

They hiked in the __ __ __ __ __ __ <u>i</u> <u>n</u> __.

A. Look at the map of Japan. Complete the sentences with the correct words from the box.

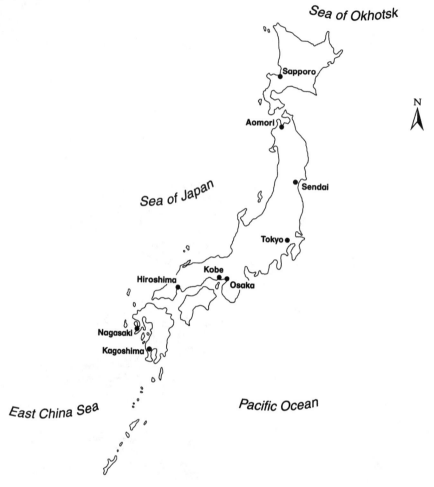

1. Japan is _____ of the Sea of Japan and _____ of the Pacific Ocean.

2. Kobe is _____ of Osaka.

3. Sapporo is _____ and _____ of Nagasaki.

4. Sendai is _____ of Aomori, but _____ of Tokyo.

B. Use the correct words from the box to complete these sentences about Japan.

1. Sapporo _____ the Sea of Japan.

2. Kobe is _____ Osaka.

3. Sendai _____ the Pacific Ocean.

4. Nagasaki isn't _____ Hiroshima, but it is _____ Kagoshima.

plane	car
train	bike
bus	motorcycle

Answer the questions using complete sentences.
Use the word *by* and words from the box.

1. How do you get to the supermarket?
   I get there by car. _____

2. How do you get from your country to the United States?
   _____

3. How did you get to school yesterday?
   _____

4. How did you and your family travel on your vacation?
   _____

5. How do you usually go to a friend's house?
   _____

PRACTICE 4

Complete Nancy's postcard with *was* or *were.*

October 12, _____

Hi, Molly

   How are you? Last week I (1.) _____ on vacation.
I went to Miami by bus to visit my grandmother.
It (2.) _____ a terrible trip. There (3.) _____
a lot of people on the bus. It (4.) _____ so hot, and
the bus (5.) _____ very small. There (6.) _____
two little boys next to me. They (7.) _____ happy
and friendly, but they talked a lot. I (8.) _____
very tired, but the bus ride (9.) _____ interesting!
(10.) _____ you on vacation last week, too?
   Write soon and tell me all about your vacation.

                                    Your friend,

                                    Nancy

Molly Peterson
_____

38 Pine Brook Drive
_____

Boulder, CO 80302
_____

_____

PRACTICE 5

A. Read Fernando's letter. Write some information questions (and answers) about Fenando's vacation. Use the simple past tense of *be* and information in the chart.

Dear Marco,

I am having a great vacation! I went to visit my friend Luisa in Chicago. She lives there. After Chicago, I went to Florida. I met Dan there. Dan and I spent one week in Florida. We were in Key West for four days, and then we went to Orlando for three days. We didn't go to Disney World, but we had a great time. We celebrated my birthday there. We went out for a great dinner! Tomorrow Dan and I are going home.

See you soon,
Fernando

How long Where	was were	Dan and Fernando at Disney World Fernando in Florida Dan and Fernando in Key West Luisa Fernando's birthday celebrated Dan and Fernando in Orlando Dan

1. _How long was Fernando in Florida_ ? _One week_
2. _____ ? _____
3. _____ ? _____
4. _____ ? _____
5. _____ ? _____

B. Use the information in Fernando's letter to write yes/no questions and answers.

1. Dan and Fernando in Miami

   Were Dan and Fernando in Miami ? _Yes, they were._

2. Dan in Chicago

   _____ ? _____

3. Dan and Fernando at Disney World

   _____ ? _____

4. Luisa in Florida

   _____ ? _____

C. Write more yes/no questions and answers.

Unit 8

60

Read each sentence. Write questions using *How long does it take* or *How long did it take.*

1. **A:** _____?

   B: It took me twenty minutes to walk to the bus stop.

2. **A:** _____?

   B: It takes three hours to get to Atlanta by train.

3. **A:** _____?

   B: It takes five minutes to get to the grocery store.

4. **A:** _____?

   B: It took her five hours to drive to El Paso.

5. **A:** _____?

   B: It took them an hour to get to the hotel.

PRACTICE 7

Listen. Circle the correct words.

1. Angelina is in	Atlanta	New York	Washington
2. Angelina traveled by	plane	plane and bus	plane and train
3. The trip took	three hours	half an hour	an hour
4. Tomorrow, Angelina will see New York by	bus	train	car
5. Angelina will call her mother on	Tuesday	Friday	Wednesday

Read the letter about Diana's vacation in Mexico. Then complete the chart.

Dear Grandpa,

We had a great time in Mexico. First we went to Mexico City. It's very big. There are so many people. We visited interesting museums and ate delicious food. Then we went to Acapulco. The beaches were beautiful, and the water was warm. We swam every day. After Acapulco, we traveled to Oaxaca. It's a lovely, old city. We bought some beautiful things there. Finally, we went to Cancun. We went to some very interesting ruins. There were a lot of tourists from different countries there. We stayed in Cancun for three days. It was very hot, but we loved every minute of the trip. I am sending you some pictures.

I have many good memories of my trip to Mexico and its warm and friendly people.

Love,
Diana

Place	Description	What she did
Mexico City		
	beautiful beaches	
		bought beautiful things
	many tourists	

Read these sentences. Does the verb agree with the subject? Five sentences have mistakes. Write those sentences correctly.

1. Joanne like to take vacations.

_____

2. Who were that?

_____

3. There was two accidents on the highway.

_____

4. I wasn't there.

_____

5. It don't rain in the winter.

_____

6. Where was she yesterday?

_____

7. They doesn't have your book.

_____

PRACTICE 10

Write a postcard to a friend about your favorite vacation.

Check Your Knowledge

Vocabulary Check

Look at the pictures. Complete the sentences with the correct words from the box.

ballet	beach	hotel	museum
ocean	bike	plane	train

1.

2.

3.

4.

5.

6.

1. Linda and her family went to Mexico by _____.
2. They stayed in a big _____.
3. They went to the _____.
4. They swam in the _____.
5. They went to an interesting _____ in Mexico City.
6. One night they went to the _____.

Check Your Understanding

A. Complete the conversations with *was* or *were*.

1. A: Where _____ you last week?

   B: I _____ on vacation with my family. We _____ in Canada.

2. A: What part of Canada _____ you in?

   B: We _____ in Calgary, Banff National Park, and Lake Louise.

3. A: Did you like it there?

   B: Yes. Lake Louise _____ really beautiful.

4. A: How long _____ you at Lake Louise?

   B: We _____ there for only two days. I _____ sad when we left.

B. Look at the pictures in **Vocabulary Check**. Did you ever visit one of these places? Write in your notebook about your trip. Use the simple past tense of *be*. (Where is it? How did you get there? How long did it take you to get there? When did you go? How long were you there? What did you do there?)

clear	stormy	snowy
cloudy	hot	warm
cold	rainy	windy

Complete the puzzle using the pictures and
the correct weather words from the box.

Across

3.

6.

7.

8.

Down

1.

2.

4.

5.

7.

PRACTICE 2

Look at the thermometers. Complete the sentences with the correct words from the box and the correct temperature.

Fahrenheit	Celsius
cool	hot
warm	cold
temperature	degrees

1. The temperature is __95__ degrees __Fahrenheit__ /36 __degrees__ Celsius. It's __hot__ .

2. The _____ is 32 _____ Fahrenheit/ 0 degrees _____. It's _____.

3. The _____ is 56 _____ _____/ _____ _____Celsius. It's _____.

4. The _____ is _____ _____ Fahrenheit/ _____ degrees _____. It's _____.

PRACTICE 3

Look at the weather chart. Answer the questions.

	New York City	Miami	Tokyo	Ecuador
Winter	❄ 34°F/2°C	68°F/20°C	43°F/5°C	🌧 55°F/13°C
Spring	🌧 58°F/15°C	🌧 71°F/23°C	59°F/16°C	🌧 58°F/15°C
Summer	☀ 88°F/60°C	☀ 98°F/37°C	🌧 75°F/24°C	57°F/14°C
Fall	60°F/16°C	70°F/22°C	56°F/14°C	58°F/15°C

KEY: Sunny ☀ Cloudy ☁ Rain 🌧 Snow ❄

1. What's the weather like in the spring in New York City? _____

2. What's the rainy season in Ecuador? _____ In Tokyo? _____

3. Does it snow in Miami? _____

4. What's the temperature in Tokyo in the winter? _____

5. Is the weather in Miami very hot in the fall? _____

6. What are the seasons like in the United States? _____

_____

7. What's the temperature like in Ecuador?_____

Look at the pictures. Respond to the questions.

1.

2.

3.

4.

1. **A:** Let's go to the park today.
   B: *We can't go to the park today. It's cold and rainy.* _____

2. **A:** Let's ride our bikes to the movies.
   B: _____

3. **A:** Let's walk to the library after school.
   B: _____

4. **A:** Let's wash the car this afternoon.
   B: _____

PRACTICE 5

Complete the conversations with the correct words from the box.

going to do	going to go
going to wear	going to be
going to stay	

1. **A:** Where is Perry _____ Friday night?
   B: She's _____ to the school dance.

2. **A:** What is she _____ to the dance?
   B: She's _____ her new red dress.

3. **A:** Where's her brother _____ Friday night?
   B: He's _____ to the movies.

4. **A:** And what are you _____ Friday night?
   B: I'm _____ home!

Unit 9

Look at the pictures. Complete the conversations. Use *going to wear* and the correct clothing words.

jacket jeans raincoat shorts

sweater T-shirt dress shirt

1. A: It's rainy and warm today. What are you going to wear to school?

B: _____

2. A: It's cold and windy outside. What are Rosa and Lucía going to wear to the mall?

B: _____

3. A: It's a cool fall day. What are you going to wear to the dance tonight?

B: _____

4. A: It's hot and sunny. What is Takashi going to wear to the park?

B: _____

Answer the questions. Use complete sentences.

1. What are you going to do this afternoon?

_____

2. What are you and your family going to do tonight?

_____

3. What are you going to wear to school tomorrow?

_____

PRACTICE 8

be	study
go	wear
play	

Complete the conversations. Use the correct form of *be*, *going to*, and the verbs in the box.

1. **A:** _____Is_____ the weather _____*going to be*_____ sunny tomorrow?

   B: Yes, it _____. Let's go to the park!

2. **A:** _____ you _____ happy after the test is over?

   B: No, I _____ not. I didn't study.

3. **A:** _____ Tara _____ to the dance Friday night?

   B: Yes, she _____. She _____ a new dress.

4. **A:** _____ Sam and Julie _____ in a band

   Saturday night?

   B: No. They _____ to a party.

5. **A:** _____ we _____ at the library tonight?

   B: Yes, we _____. I need your help with my science report.

PRACTICE 9

Listen to the weather forecast. Complete the chart.

National Weather Forecast

City	Weather	Low Temperature	High Temperature
1. Boston	clear and cool	42°	62°
2. Miami			
3. New Orleans			
4. Seattle			
5. Los Angeles			
6. Honolulu			
7. Anchorage			

Read the weather report. Then use the symbols to complete the weather map.
Write the symbols and the temperatures on the map.

SUNDAY GAZETTE

Weather Forecast

Tomorrow the northeast is going to be cold and cloudy. The high temperature in Maine is going to be about 45 degrees Fahrenheit. The south is going to be warm and sunny. The high temperature in Florida is going to be about 85 degrees Fahrenheit. The mountains in the west are going to get a lot of snow tomorrow, but it isn't going to be very cold. The low temperature in Colorado is going to be about 30 degrees Fahrenheit. In the north the weather is going to be very stormy. It isn't going to snow, but Minnesota is going to get a lot of rain.

KEY: Sunny   Cloudy   Rain   Snow

PRACTICE 11

Find the eight misspelled words and spell them correctly.

   The wether yesterday was very bad. There was a big snowstrom. All of the shools were closed. The mathers and fathers were unhappy, but the childrun were happy. They plaied in the snow all day. Today it is suny. The parents are smilieing again.

1. _____   4. _____   7. _____

2. _____   5. _____   8. _____

3. _____   6. _____

PRACTICE 12

Look at the map and write a weather report for tomorrow about the cities in the box.

Tomorrow's Weather Forecast

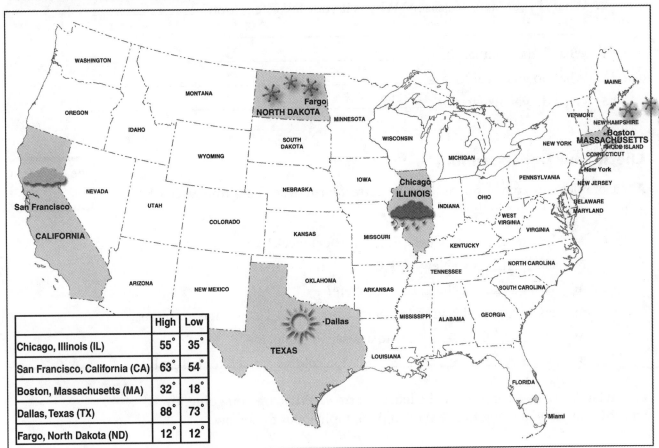

	High	Low
Chicago, Illinois (IL)	55°	35°
San Francisco, California (CA)	63°	54°
Boston, Massachusetts (MA)	32°	18°
Dallas, Texas (TX)	88°	73°
Fargo, North Dakota (ND)	12°	12°

Tomorrow it's going to _____

_____

_____

_____

_____

Unit 9

71

 # Check Your Knowledge

Vocabulary Check

Name your favorite season. What is the weather like? Use the words in the box to help you answer the questions.

cloudy	cold	hot	clear
snowy	rainy	windy	sunny

1. Where do you live? _____

2. What is your favorite season? Why is it your favorite season? _____

_____

3. What is the weather like? _____

4. What do you wear? _____

5. What do you like to do? _____

Check Your Understanding

be	go
do	see

A. Complete the conversations. Use the correct form of *be*, the future with *going to*, and the verbs in the box.

1. A: Where _____ Chen _____ next week?

   B: He _____ to New York City.

2. A: What _____ he _____ there?

   B: He _____ his grandparents. They _____ to some museums.

3. A: _____ they _____ to a baseball game, too?

   B: No, they _____. It _____ too cold next week for baseball.

B. What is the weather going to be like tomorrow? What are you going to wear? What are you going to do? Write a paragraph about tomorrow.

_____

_____

_____

_____

_____

PRACTICE 1

Look at the pictures. Write the kind of show under the pictures. Use words from the box.

Kinds of TV Shows

sitcom	cartoon
drama	news
sports show	game show
soap opera	talk show

1. _____

2. _____

3. _____

4. _____

5. _____

6. _____

7. _____

8. _____

Look at the pictures. Complete the sentences with the correct words.

1.

2.

3.

4.

5.

6.

1. The _____ in the commercial is smiling.
   actor/actress

2. The game show _____ is winning a lot of money.
   contestant/reporter

3. The _____ is playing soccer.
   athlete/actor

4. This _____ is talking to a police officer.
   contestant/reporter

5. The talk show _____ is talking about three guests.
   host/contestant

6. The _____ is visiting the talk show.
   host/guest

Read the TV guide. Then write the names of the shows.

Monday, August 3 Afternoon Programs		
3:00	5	**Mid-afternoon News**
	7	**All Our Days** Alex tells Tina that he is going to marry Sandy.
	9	**Cartoon Carnival**
3:30	5	**Baseball** New York Yankees vs. Los Angeles Dodgers
	7	**Would You Like to Have $1,000,000?**
	9	**Let's Talk! with Rita Harris** Rita's guest is actor Rod Norman
4:00	7	**Emergency!** Sam and Dave try to save a young girl in a fire.
5:00	5	**Everyone Loves Lucy** Lucy tries to learn to swim.
	7	**Sports Roundup with Dick West** Baseball coach Greg Dunbar is Dick's guest.
	9	**Guess That Price**

Sitcom   _____   News   _____

Sports   _____*Baseball*_____   Talk show   _____

   _____   Cartoon   _____

Game shows   _____   Drama   _____

   _____   Soap opera   _____

PRACTICE 4

Complete the sentences with *in*, *on*, or *at*.

LISA: What's **(1.)** _____ TV?

DAD: I'm watching the news **(2.)** _____ Channel 5. There was a big snowstorm **(3.)** _____ Chicago.

LISA: What else is **(4.)** _____?

DAD: Look **(5.)** _____ the TV guide.

LISA: Where's the TV guide?

DAD: It's there **(6.)** _____ the table.

LISA: Well, there's a game show that started **(7.)** _____ 4:30.

DAD: I like the news. Let's leave the TV **(8.)** _____ this station.

LISA: What's **(9.)** _____ after the news?

DAD: **(10.)** _____ 6:00, there's a new sitcom called *Tom's World*. I read a good review of it **(11.)** _____ the paper. Let's watch that.

LISA: OK. It sounds fine to me.

PRACTICE 5

Complete the conversation with the correct object pronouns from the box.

her	him
me	them
us	you
it	

ANN: Hi, Nora. What happened on *All Our Days* yesterday? I wasn't home.

NORA: Maria told Tony she didn't want **(1.)** _____ to be her boyfriend. He got angry and left. Then he went to John and Marsha's house. He told **(2.)** _____ what happened.

ANN: Oh, no! Then what?

NORA: I don't know. My mother called **(3.)** _____ on the phone, so I didn't see the end of the show. But I know Sarah taped **(4.)** _____ on her VCR.

ANN: Can you call Sarah? I know she likes **(5.)** _____. We are all good friends! Can you ask **(6.)** _____ to give **(7.)** _____ the tape?

NORA: I called Sarah after the show. She came to my house and gave **(8.)** _____ the tape. I can give **(9.)** _____ the tape tomorrow after school.

ANN: Great! It was nice of Sarah to give **(10.)** _____ the tape first. I *know* Paula and Ginny want to see the show, too.

NORA: I know you're right about that! See **(11.)** _____ tomorrow. Bye!

Complete the sentences with the correct word or words.

ALMA: I have my pictures here from my trip to Turkey.

BRIAN: Really? Could you show them **(1.)** _____?
me/to me

ALMA: Sure, I'd love to.

BRIAN: Wait a minute. Here comes Edgar. I know he wants to see your

pictures, too.

ALMA: OK. I can show **(2.)** _____ **(3.)** _____ at the
them/to them   him/to him

same time.

BRIAN: Wow! This is a beautiful picture of a mosque. Where is it?

ALMA: It's the Mosque of Suleiman I in Istanbul. Isn't it great?

EDGAR: Did you know Susan is doing a report on Istanbul? Can you show

(4.) _____ this picture?
her/to her

ALMA: I can show **(5.)** _____ **(6.)** _____ later this
it/to it   her/to her

afternoon. I have to go to English class now. I'll show

(7.) _____ the rest of my photos later, too.
you/to you

PRACTICE **7**

Listen to the commercials. What does each commercial tell about? Write the
correct letters on the lines.

Commercial 1 _____
Commercial 2 _____
Commercial 3 _____
Commercial 4 _____
Commercial 5 _____
Commercial 6 _____

a.

b.

c.

d.

e.

f.

Read the summary of the television shows. Then answer the questions.

Summary of *Life and Love*

Clara and Martin decided to get married, but they didn't tell their parents. Ricky told Sara that he didn't love her. He told her that he loved Monica. Sara got angry and pushed him. He fell and hit his head. She called an ambulance. The doctors took him to the hospital. Monica went to see him, but he didn't know her.

Summary of *For the Good Times*

Larry decided to go to California on vacation. He asked Nancy to go with him. She said, "Yes." She was so excited. Jerry gave Ramona a present. Mike was very angry, so he showed Ramona a letter Jerry wrote to him. Then Ramona went to look for Jerry.

1. What kind of show is *Life and Love*? _____
2. What did Clara and Martin do? _____
3. What happened to Ricky? _____
4. What did Larry decide to do? _____
5. Why is Nancy excited? _____
6. Why did Ramona go to look for Jerry? _____

PRACTICE 9

Read this summary of a television show. Rewrite it in the present or the past tense.

      Dave sees a car accident. He called an ambulance. Then he tries to help the people. The driver of the car was his best friend, Sam. Dave's girlfriend, Nora, is in the car, too. Sam was very upset. Then the ambulance arrives. They took Sam and Nora to the hospital. Dave goes to the hospital, too.

_____

_____

_____

_____

_____

_____

_____

_____

_____

PRACTICE 10

Write a summary of your favorite television show. Use either the present tense or the past tense. (Don't mix tenses.)

_____

_____

_____

_____

_____

_____

_____

_____

_____

✓ Check Your Knowledge

Vocabulary Check

Complete the sentences with the correct words from the box.

actors	commercial	game show	news reporter
sports show	athletes	drama	guest
soap opera	talk show	cartoon	sitcom

1. Sandy is watching a program about the work of police officers. The _____, called *Police Stories,* is on TV every Friday night. The _____ on the show are Greg Reed and Jack Factor.

2. Laura is watching *A Dream for Tomorrow.* She watches it every day. The stories make her cry a lot. Sometimes they make her angry. Sometimes famous people spend time on this _____. Then it's really exciting to watch!

3. Yoshi is watching a _____ called *Meet the People.* The _____ is talking about his family.

4. The Fisher Family is watching a _____. The _____ on the show are playing volleyball.

Check Your Understanding

Complete the sentences with the correct word or words.

JOHN: You didn't give (1.) _____ my magazines.
                                  me/to me

EVAN: Yes, I did! I gave (2.) _____ (3.) _____ last night.
                              them/to them   **you/to you**

JOHN: No, you didn't! Mario wanted to see (4.) _____. You gave
                                              them/to them

the magazines (5.) _____.
                    him/to him

EVAN: You are right. I'm sorry.

WHO WON THE GAME?

PRACTICE 1

Match the sentences with the pictures.

_____ **1.** The score is tied.

_____ **2.** She thinks swimming is hard.

_____ **3.** These people think this baseball game is boring.

_____ **4.** This baseball game is exciting.

_____ **5.** The football game was dangerous.

_____ **6.** The Lions are winning the soccer game.

_____ **7.** They think playing chess is interesting.

_____ **8.** They think swimming is fun.

a.

b.

c.

d.

e.

f.

g.

h.

PRACTICE 2

Look at the pictures. Complete the sentences with activities and words from the box.

fun	exciting
interesting	great exercise
easy	boring
boring	hard
dangerous	

1. Mrs. Wilson and her daughter like to _____shop_____ at the mall. They think it's _____fun_____. Mr. Wilson thinks it's _____.

2. Tom and Julia like to _____. They think it's _____.

3. The children like to _____ in winter. They think it's _____.

4. The students like to _____ on a very hot day. They think it's _____.

5. Sam likes to _____ after school. He thinks it's _____.

6. Raymond likes to _____ with his brother. He thinks it's _____, but it's _____.

7. Students like to _____ on Friday nights. They think it's _____.

Look at the pictures. What do the people think about their activities? Complete
the conversations. Use words from the box in Practice 2.

1. Brian   Ted

2. Mrs. Wilson   Mr. Wilson

3. Melinda   Juan

4. Carl   Paul

Complete the sentences. Use activity words from the box in Practice 5.

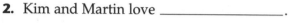

1. Pablo likes to _____ in his free time.

2. Kim and Martin love _____.

3. Some people love _____.

4. What do you like to do in your free time?

_____.

_____.

PRACTICE 5

Make sentences. Use *it's* and adjective infinitives.

It's	exciting fun dangerous interesting boring easy hard	to	play baseball ski watch television play chess swim ice skate ride a bike

1. *It's fun to swim.* _____

2. _____

3. _____

4. _____

PRACTICE 6

Change the sentences in Practice 5. Now use the verb + *–ing* as a noun.

1. *Swimming is fun.* _____

2. _____

3. _____

4. _____

PRACTICE 7

Complete these sentences. Use the infinitive form of the verb or the verb + *-ing* as a noun.

1. I think it's fun _____.

2. I love _____.

3. I don't like _____.

4. My friends and I think _____ is boring.

5. I think it's easy _____.

6. My parents think _____ is dangerous.

7. My teacher says _____ is important.

8. I think it's difficult _____.

PRACTICE 8

Write questions using an *-ing* form of the verbs. Then write a short answer giving your own opinion. You can use words from the box.

boring	hard
easy	exciting
dangerous	interesting
fun	

1. like/play volleyball

A: *Do you like playing volleyball?* _____

B: *Yes, I do.* **OR** *No, I don't. I think it's hard.* _____

2. like/watch movies

A: _____

B: _____

3. think/play tennis/is easy

A: _____

B: _____

4. think/shop/is fun

A: _____

B: _____

5. like/go to concerts

A: _____

B: _____

6. like/eat at restaurants

A: _____

B: _____

7. like/cook dinner

A: _____

B: _____

PRACTICE 9

Listen. Circle the correct words and complete the sentences.

1. Katie **(likes/doesn't like)** _____.
   She thinks it's _____.

2. Mark and Al **(like/don't like)** _____.
   They think it's _____.

3. Sara **(likes/doesn't like)** _____.
   She thinks it's _____.

4. They decided to go _____.
   They think it's _____.

PRACTICE 10

Read the newspaper article about the basketball game. Then answer the questions.

Bears Defeat Tigers

The Bears played a great basketball game in Derby Gymnasium last night. It was the most exciting game of the season. They played against the Tigers, who won the state championship last year. Most of the players on the Tigers played on last year's team, so they have a lot of experience.

Coach Grisham told the Bears before the game, "You are a great team. You can win this game if you play hard." He was right. At the end of the first half the score was tied 38–38. Then, in the second half, the Tigers started very strong. They scored 10 points in the first five minutes. Then the Bears' captain, Ben Foster, called a time out and talked to his teammates. After that, they played really well. At the end of the game, the score was Bears 76–Tigers 68. Congratulations to the Bears for a great team effort!

1. What sport is this article about? _____

2. What are the names of the teams? _____

3. Who won the state championship last year? _____

4. What was the score at the end of the first half of the game?_____

5. Who is Ben Foster? _____

6. Why did Ben Foster call a "time out"? _____

Correct these sentences. Use punctuation, quotation marks and capital letters.

1. The coach said don't be late

_____

2. Mrs. morris asked what time does the game begin

_____

3. Sam said I never go biking in the snow

_____

4. We lost the game nora said

_____

5. He said this game is boring

_____

PRACTICE 12

Read the information below about a soccer game. Write a sports article about the game.

What happened?	soccer game
When?	yesterday afternoon
Score:	Franklin High School 4
	Lincoln High School 2
Who scored goals?	For Franklin High: Edgar Ruiz 2 goals, Nabil Jabba 2 goals
	For Lincoln High: Antonio Corelli 1 goal, Karl Nelson 1 goal

_____

_____

_____

_____

_____

_____

_____

 **Check Your Knowledge**

Vocabulary Check

Complete the sentences. Use some words from the box to describe the pictures.

boring	chess	skiing
exciting	fun	winning
hard	losing	tennis
ice skating		

1. **A:** What's the score of the Chicago Bulls game?

   B: The Bulls are _____. The score is _____ to _____. It's _____ to watch.

2. **A:** What's the score of the Los Angeles Lakers game?

   B: The Lakers are _____. The score is _____ to _____. It's _____ watch.

3. **A:** Do you like _____?

   B: No, I don't. It's too _____ to go down the mountains.

4. **A:** Do you like _____?

   B: Yes, I do. It's _____!

5. **A:** Do you like _____?

   B: No, I don't. It's _____ to stand and not fall down.

Check Your Understanding

A. Write a sentence with *it's* and the words.

   1. dangerous/play hockey _____.

   2. boring/watch golf on TV _____.

B. Change the sentences in Part A. Use the verb + *–ing* as a noun.

   1. dangerous/play hockey _____.

   2. boring/watch golf on TV _____.

PRACTICE 1

Name the parts of the newspaper. Use the correct words from the box.

ad	article
column	comic strip
front page	headline
photograph	

1. _____

2. _____

3. _____

4. _____

5. _____

6. _____

7. _____

The Wildcat Review

Wildcat Prom This Friday

The Westville High School will host its 20th Senior Prom this Friday, May 23rd. The prom, sponsored by the Senior Class, is sure to please all Wildcat students and their guests from start to finish.

Janie Kang and Sam Hunt will be crowned Prom Queen and King.

This year's prom features the music of The Beat, a band that's long been a favorite of

Ben Moran

People have been telling us all week long to go to the Wildcat Prom this Friday. But why should we go? Everyone spends so much money and energy on this one party that it's almost a certainty that the evening won't match your expectations. Phooey!

Still, there's a certain magic to it all ... the fine and beautiful clothes, the flowers, the fancy food and music and decoration, the fun. So don't miss it!

TONY'S FORMALS

Great Tuxes Still Available!

Call: **555–2300**

The Bookworm
in the Oaks Mall

20% OFF Special Sale on Books!

Look at the pictures. Write the names of the people who work on a newspaper.

cartoonist	columnist
editor	photographer
writer	reporter

1. _____

2. _____

3. _____

Fire on Front Street

Lori Ames

There was a big fire at 66 Front Street yesterday afternoon. No one was home at the time. A neighbor saw smoke and called the fire department. The fire fighters arrived about 2:30.

4. _____

5. _____

PRACTICE 3

What do these people do? Complete the sentences.

1. A reporter _____.

2. A writer _____.

3. A photographer _____.

4. An editor _____.

5. A cartoonist _____.

Read the article. Write the correct form of the verbs.

The Wildcat Review wants **(1. hear)** _____ from Westville High School students about the interesting things that go on in the high school each week. Please **(2. tell)** _____ your news to any of the paper's reporters. We **(3. wait)** _____ to hear from you! You can read about two of our reporters right here.

Raúl Meléndez **(4. be)** _____ the sports reporter for the newspaper. He **(5. attend)** _____ many sporting events each week. He **(6. write)** _____ three articles last week about our swimming, baseball, and volleyball teams. Next week he **(7. write)** _____ about a baseball game with Stevenson High School and a tennis tournament.

Joy Kapila **(8. be)** _____ the editor of the paper last year. This year she **(9. take)** _____ our photographs. Tomorrow afternoon Joy **(10. take)** _____ a picture of the Westville Honor Society. This photograph **(11. be)** _____ in our newspaper next week. Look for it!

Change the statements into yes/no questions.

The teachers went home early.

1. *Did the teachers go home early?* _____

Sam and Mike are going to leave tomorrow.

2. _____?

She went by bus.

3. _____?

They were in Paris last summer.

4. _____?

The game was exciting.

5. _____?

PRACTICE 6

Write questions about the underlined words.

1. *Why does John want to be the editor of the newspaper?*

   John wants to be the editor of the newspaper <u>because he likes to write</u>.

2. _____ ?

   The soccer game was <u>boring</u>.

3. _____ ?

   Frank works <u>at a drugstore</u> on the weekend.

4. _____ ?

   Karen <u>practices piano</u> after school.

PRACTICE 7

Listen to the news reports. Complete the chart. Write the letter of the best headline for each report.

News Report	Kind of Report (review, sports, weather or city news)	Headline
1		
2		
3		
4		
5		

Headlines

a. Basco Wins Election

b. Night of Horrors — Boring!

c. Dolphins End with Win

d. **Rain to Come Tomorrow**

e. Fire Burns Factory

PRACTICE 8

This paragraph has ten errors in spelling, punctuation, capitalization, and grammar. Circle them and then rewrite the paragraph correctly.

Nancy Robinson is a new student in our School. she moved here from texas two months ago. She says, Alaska is very different from Texas but I really like it. For example, in Texas, Nancy never sees snow and it was very flat. I really like the high mountains here in Alaska, she said. They're very beautiful. Nancy likes to riding horses and going biking. She also play basketball.

_____

_____

_____

Read Robert's notes for a newspaper article. Then write an article about the school election from the notes.

What?   School president election next week
Who?   The two candidates: Tony Jaffe and
          Jennifer Ramos
When?   Tuesday, 9:00 to 1:00
Where?   School cafeteria
Why vote for Tony or Jennifer?
Tony Jaffe: "I want to be your president. I am going to help make the food better in the cafeteria."
Jennifer Ramos: "It's exciting to hear all of your ideas. I want to make them work when I'm president!"

_____
_____
_____
_____
_____
_____
_____

Write a newspaper article about a new student or an event at your school. Check your writing when you're finished. (Look at the STRATEGY on page 126 in your Student Book.)

_____
_____
_____
_____
_____
_____

Check Your Knowledge

Vocabulary Check

Complete each sentence with a word from the box that names the correct part of the newspaper.

ad	photograph
article	review
comic strip	weather report

1. Paulina read the _____ about the cheerleaders first.

2. Next she looked at the _____ of the cheerleaders.

3. After that she read the _____ because she wants to buy a TV.

4. She loves to read the cartoons the best, so she saved the _____ for last.

Monday

Cheerleaders can't toss

Cheerleaders at Truman High will do their last tossing stunt on January 15.

On January 15, all high school cheerleaders in the state of Illinois are going to stop tossing one another up in the air. Cheerleaders often do this stunt at basketball games. School principal Fred Curtis wants this change because he doesn't want anyone to get hurt. Mr. Curtis and other school officials say that cheerleading is not a sport and that cheerleaders need to lead cheers at school games.

Electronics City

SALE on all TVs and CD Players

Sale ends
Saturday, January 16

Check Your Understanding

A. Read the newspaper page in **Vocabulary Check**. Answer the questions in complete sentences.

1. When are the Truman High cheerleaders going to do their last tossing stunt?

   _____

2. Why does Fred Curtis want cheerleaders to stop tossing?

   _____

3. Where is there a sale on TVs?

   _____

B. Write a short review of a movie or a TV show you watched or a book you read. Answer these questions.

What is it about? Did you like it? Why or why not?

_____

_____

_____